KT-474-087

59

PARIS

Nathalie Mont-Servan

PARIS

Illustrations by Louis Monier

GRÜND

CONTENTS

Designed by Jean-Pierre Rosier

Première édition 1984 by Librairie Gründ, Paris
© texte: 1984 Librairie Gründ, Paris
© illustrations: 1984 Librairie Gründ, Paris

ISBN 2-7000-5158-0

Dépôt légal: mars 1984
Produced by Mandarin Offset
Printed and bound in Hong Kong

Endpapers: The Seine...Bridges...Houses-...The Eiffel Tower.

Half-title: Place Saint-André-des-Arts (6e)

Title: The Seine and the Pont-Neuf; on the left, the Quai des Grands-Augustins; on the right, the Louvre.

Page 4: A typical aerial view of Paris rooftops; in the background, on the right, the Hôtel de Ville.

A classical mythological scene, typical of the Jardin des Tuileries.

A few important dates

53 BC Earliest written reference to Lutetia and its inhabitants, the Parisii, in Julius Caesar's Gallic Wars.

360 AD Lutetia is renamed Paris.

451 Paris is saved from Attila and his Huns by Saint Geneviève's Prayers. She becomes the city's patron saint.

508 After his victory at Soissons, Clovis established Paris at his capital. Since then the city has been the political centre of France.

861 Paris invaded by the Normans.

987 Hugues Capet settled at the Palais de la Cité.

1108 Louis VI created an administration for Paris, headed by a Provost.

1190-1210 Philippe-Auguste gave an impetus to the future development of Paris – the royal city around the Louvre, the commercial centre by the Hôtel de Ville and the University of Paris on the Left Bank. His fortified walls marked the boundaries of the city.

1163-1330 Construction of Notre-Dame Cathedral.

1365 Beginning of the construction of the Bastille, and development of the Saint-Antoine and Saint-Paul districts.

1430 Joan of Arc tried to recover Paris from the English who had occupied it since 1420.

1533 François I laid the foundation stone of the Hôtel de Ville. The siting chosen for the gateway of the Louvre would affect the layout of modern Paris – right up to La Défense.

1564 Construction of the Palais des Tuileries by Catherine de Medici, mother of Charles IX.

1578 Henri III began building the Pont-Neuf, connecting the Right Bank to the Faubourg Saint-Germain.

1594 Henri IV settled in Paris. He created the Place Royale and undertook great building works including the Smaritaine hydraulic system for the supply of water to the Right Bank. His widow, Marie de Medici, built the Palais de Luxembourg.

1629 Under Louis XIII, creation of the Académie Française, the Jardin des Plantes, the Val-de-Grâce, the Palais Cardinal by Richelieu (Palais-Royal).

1649 Louis XIV left Paris after the Fronde uprising. The King and the Court would not return to town until the Revolution.

1664 Colbert commissioned Perrault, Mansart, Le Nôtre and other artists of the period to design and build many monuments, gardens, bridges and triumphal arches.

1720 Under the Regency and Louis XV building increased greatly. Street names began to be displayed on stone plaques. Follies such as the Quartier Gaillon were built in open country.

1784 Reign of Louis XVI. Building of the sixth encircling wall, known as the Fermiers Généraux, which was intended to prevent tax evasion.

1789 The Revolution treated the property of monasteries and emigrés as national property and sold it to speculators.

1800 Napoléon gave Paris an administration controlled by the Prefects of Paris and of the Seine.

1814-1815 The Russian, English and Prussian Allies pitched their camps on the Champs-Elysées.

1815-1829 Waterloo. Louis XVIII continued the work of his predecessors. Charles X introduced gas-lighting.

1830-1848 Louis-Philippe erected the obelisk from Luxor on the Place de la Concorde. He brought home Napoleon's ashes and placed them in the Invalides.

1852-1869 With the support of Napoleon III, Baron Haussmann transformed Old Paris into the City of Light.

1870 The imperial government overthrown af-

Viewed from the Napoleon courtyard, the Louvre Pyramid - designed by the architect I.M. Peï - lifts its unspoilt lines along the Bastille-Défense axis. Its 612 glass diamond-shaped facets are cleaned by teams of roped "mountaineers". Inaugurated by President Mitterrand in 1988, it tops the main entrance to the museum and contrasts with the baroque statue of Louis XIV by Le Bernin, by which visitors queue up.

ter the surrender of Sedan. The Third Republic Proclaimed. Paris under 4 months' seige during avery severe winter.

1871 The capital's monuments suffered severely under the Commune. Insurgents set fire to the Hôtel de Ville, the Tuileries, the Library of the Louvre and to many of the private houses in the Faubourg St Germain.

1879 The Government returned to Paris from Versailles and began reconstructing the monuments and buildings destroyed in 1871. Sacré-Cœur was built in Montmartre by national subscription.

1900 Opening of the Metro for the World Exhibition, which left behind monuments ans new districts especially to the west : The Pont Alexandre III, the Grand and Petit Palais all bear witness to their splendour.

1913 Construction of the Champs-Élysées Theatre.

1914 Paris, saved by the "Taxis of the Marne" bringing in reinforcements to the battle.

1918 Signing of the Armistice on November 11th.

1919 On 14 July, a procession from the Porte Maillot to the Place de la République celebrated Victory and Peace.

1920 11 November : the unknown soldier was buried under the Arc de Triomphe.

1925 Exhibition of Decorative Arts.

1931 The Colonial Exhibition held in the Bois de Vincennes. Creation of the Musée de la France d'Outre-Mer, now known as the Musée des Arts Africains et Océaniens.

1937 International Exhibition of Arts and Techniques. The Palais de Chaillot and its fountains replaced Trocadéro.

1939-1940 Beginning of the Second World War. The Germans invaded France on 10 May and Paris was declared an open city on 14 June.

1944 20 August. An armistice is negotiated between the Swedish consul Raoul Nordling and General von Choltitz. On 25 August the Leclerc division, the U.S. army and Général de Gaulle entered Paris to great popular enthusiasm.

1957 Work starting on the new "LaDéfense" district with the National Centre for Industries and Techniques. The underground rail system will come in 1970 with the flourishing of office blocks as a result. The Great Arch is to culminate the whole perspective.

1969 The Halles Market is transferred to Rungis, outside Paris, and thus makes way for the Forum des Halles.

1972 The RER (high-speed underground train service) links Saint-Germain-en-Laye to Notre-Dame in 30 minutes).

1977 Inauguration of the Georges Pompidou National Art and Culture Centre, known as the Beaubourg Centre.
Paris once again elects its mayor via general election.

1981 The TGV (express train) connects Lyons to Paris in two and a half hours. Its progression throughout the country will change the face of Paris railway stations.

1984 The Bercy multi-purpose sports stadium hallmarks the opening up towards the east of the city.

1988 The Louvre Pyramid renews the layout of the "world's greatest museum".

1989 The Bastille - La Défense axis ends with the Great Arch, rising up from its concrete foundations.

199_ Work starting on the Seine Left Bank district (13th) ... to be completed in 2010.

INTRODUCTION

Flows the Seine...

"Under the Mirabeau bridge flows the Seine", sang the poet Guillaume Apollinaire, who described in verse the long journey of the river through Paris. Some days it is grey, others greenish or shimmering, and it seems to enfold the town.

Paris, past and future, has its roots under the foundations of Notre-Dame and around the Seine. Indeed, this mound rising from a swamp and called Lutetia long before the Roman conquest, was one of the islands of the river. The most important of these islands became the Cité around the site of what is now the Square de l'Evêché. Its inhabitants were called the Parisii and were part of the Celtic tribe of the Senons who were hunters, fishermen and boatmen. They soon gave their name to the city which grew up around the river. At first the city spread along the left bank of the river where the Romans had built their Forum and baths (the remains of which can still be seen in the Musée de Cluny), the first fortifications and the straight roads leading to Rome and to the boundaries of their Empire.

The magic of Paris

No city in the world has attracted so many painters, poets, writers and singers as Paris. And this magnetism has lasted 2000 years. Yesterday it inspired paintings, drawings and engravings; today photographs, video tapes, records, films and

Above: A bas-relief originally from the Church of Saint-Julien-Le-Pauvre, built into the lintel of a house in Rue Galande (5ᵉ). It represents the legend of Saint Julian the Hospitaller.

Left: The quadrilateral heart of Paris seen from Notre-Dame's Tower: the Seine between the Petit Pont and the Pont Saint-Michel. On the right, the corner of the Préfecture de Police. On the Left Bank, old, restored buildings, usually with three or four floors, the upper two set back.

T.V. broadcasts. The "City of Light" has thus become a second home to all its visitors.

Alone among the great capital cities of Europe, Paris has preserved its network of medieval streets and alleys leading into enclosed squares.

The Roman town was followed by a walled city. The first fortifications worth noting were those built by Philippe-Auguste who settled at the Louvre around 1200. They inspired Victor Hugo with a "Gothic" vision of the city in his novel *The Hunchback of Notre-Dame*:

"Seen from a bird's eye view, the three boroughs – the Cité, the University and the town – appear as a network of inextricably interwoven streets."

This impression still prevails today around the main axes: north-south from the Porte Saint-Martin to the Porte Saint-Jacques, and from the Porte Saint-Denis to the Porte Saint-Michel; and east-west from the Porte Saint-Honoré to the Porte Saint-Antoine on the Right Bank, and from the Porte Saint-Germain to the Porte Saint-Victor on the Left Bank. This tight web was, at the time of Philippe-Auguste, the only structured element in an oval labyrinth, surrounded by fields and villages.

The beginnings of geometrical urbanization

The architects and engineers of the Enlightenment strove relentlessly to put some sort of order into this medieval city with its incredible jumble of turrets and bell-towers. The only open spaces

9

were a few large gardens belonging to convents and palaces, mostly located near the fortifications. Already, by the end of the 17th century, urban geometry had begun to transform the city with the creation of the Place des Victoires, the Place Vendôme, and, a century later, the crescent-shaped Place de l'Odéon on the Left Bank.

François I, creator of the line from the Louvre to La Défense

François I (1533) can be held responsible for the orientation of Paris towards the west, more precisely towards what is now the Place de la Défense. When he undertook to embellish the Louvre, the King orientated his plans on the postern known as the gateway of Paris, and shut off the rear which was cluttered with dark alleys. His successors followed his plans, building the Palais des Tuileries, developing the Place Louis XV and extending the Champs-Elysées gardens all the way to the Arc de Triomphe, a task completed under Louis-Philippe in 1836.

Haussmann: parks and boulevards

Baron Haussmann was Prefect of Paris for seven-

teen years under Napoleon III. With the Emperor's total support, he set about reshaping Old Paris into a "City of Light" by designing broad vistas throughout the town. He constructed the new Opera, monumental railway stations and whole new districts. He tore down old buildings on the Ile de la Cité and erected an administrative centre facing Notre-Dame (which had been restored by Viollet-le-Duc). At the same time, communes and villages on the outskirts were incorporated into Paris: by 1860 the total area of the capital had increased to about 7800 hectares. In addition, new parks and green areas were added. Napoleon III had a taste for London parks, and he asked Baron Haussmann to create as much breathing space as possible by remodelling the Bois de Boulogne as an English park, by laying out parks at Buttes-Chaumont and Montsouris, and by constructing numerous squares.

As a reaction to the devastation caused by the Commune and its fierce repression by the "Versaillais" (restored government), the nation decided to build the church of Sacré-Coeur on the Butte Montmartre. By the end of the 19th century Paris had recovered its brilliance and was beginning to attract increasing numbers of visitors, especially in 1900 for the World Exhibition and the inauguration of the Metro.

The Cité, the Pointe du Vert-Galant and the Pont-Neuf. The bridge, completed during Henri IV's reign, spans the two arms of the Seine. On the Left Bank, the quai becomes a promenade, and turns into a garden near the Rue des Fossés-Saint-Bernard and the Jardin des Plantes.

Sky-scrapers

After the First World War the Art Nouveau and Floral styles gave way to the geometric designs (Art Deco) launched by the Exhibition of Decorative Arts in 1925. The Palais de Chaillot on its hillside symbolized the "Arts and Techniques" Exhibition of 1937 for which it was built.

The Second World War and the German occupation brought building to a halt in the capital, but it gathered speed again in the late fifties: in 1959, the palais du C.N.I.T., a giant triangle of glass and steel, sprang up at the Rond-Point de la Défense. But very soon it was overtaken by the tower blocks built despite many protests, in particular against the Maine-Montparnasse building which was completed as recently as 1974.

Above: Following the line Louvre–Arc de Triomphe de l'Etoile, the hill runs down towards the Porte Maillot, Neuilly, Courbevoie and Puteaux, where the Défense district has been developed since 1957. Triangular in shape, the glass, concrete and steel Palais du C.N.I.T. rests on three supports.

Left: The Champs-Elysées: one of the most famous thoroughfares in the capital, whose vista begins at the Louvre and ends at the Arc de Triomphe. Many luxury shops are to be found in the shopping arcades, recalling the early 19th century "passages".

13

PARIS AND THE SEINE

Paris and the Seine

Paris is located on the banks of the Seine, in the heartland of the largest plateau area in France. It is shaped like a basin, and two other rivers, the Marne and the Oise, converge upon it. The Marne meets the Seine upstream from the capital, near Charenton-le-Pont, and the Oise meets it in the north on the Saint-Denis side. Downstream the river wanders gently past the islands towards the sea. Rouen serves as its river port at the head of the estuary; Le Havre and Antifer are its sea ports.

The Paris Basin stretches 650 kilometres from the Cotentin peninsula in the west to Alsace in the east, and 550 kilometres from the flatlands of Flanders to the foothills of the Massif Central. It is a vast oval depression surrounded by ancient hills with piled up strata of sandstone, clay or, most frequently, limestone. Geologically, the earliest formations date from the secondary period with sediments from the tertiary. The escarpments jut out in an arc dominating a long hollow.

Ile-de-France

Paris is the centre of a region called Ile-de-France, which consists of five agricultural areas that spread out between the rivers Seine, Marne, Ourcq, Aisne and Oise. Only the communes which were part of the Carolingian Dukedom in the 9th century appear under this region's name: Roissy-en-France, the site of the Charles de Gaulle airport, is the best-known example.

The agricultural regions are closely related to the

Above: Under the Pont de la Concorde, barges carrying gravel and coal moored next to pleasure boats used as floating homes.

Left: Barges moored at the Quai des Grands-Augustins, near the place Saint-Michel. Their presence testifies to the importance of river traffic which has increased continually since the days of Lutetia, making the capital a principal port of France.

capital's everyday life: they have always supplied Paris with its food, and their people have come to live in it. Indeed, many nearby ancient villages were incorporated into Paris during the Second Empire thus doubling its area to 7800 hectares. Today, the Ile-de-France region spreads roughly over the eight original departments and its boundaries extend 200 kilometres from Notre-Dame. It has 16,500,000 inhabitants, one-third of the total French population.

The climate is mild; prevailing winds blow from the west bringing rain at all seasons. Recently, the Seine and the Marne overflowed once again in spite of dams on the Marne, between Saint-Dizier and Vitry-le-François, and on the Seine, near Troyes.

Paris-les-Iles

The Seine is the most important river link north of the Loire. It has been well canalized so as to maintain a sufficient draught at all times for its considerable barge traffic, and it makes Paris the most important port in France.

Upstream from Paris the Seine meets the Yonne at Montereau, the Marne between Charenton and Maisons-Alfort, and downstream, the Oise at Conflans-Sainte-Honorine, a charming port for barges.

In the capital, the river-banks have been canalized by the quais. During flooding, for which they are partly responsible, they hinder the fall in the water level.

The history of Paris began on the islands located in the river's winding course: called Lutetia by the Parisii and the Romans, the Cité was connected to

Between the Pont de la Concorde and the Pont des Invalides, barges at anchor on the Right Bank. In the middle, a boatman carrying his car on top of his barge passes a pleasure steamer. This area offers one of the most beautiful walks in Paris starting from the wharf at the Pont de l'Alma. In the background, the Chambre des Députés, the Hôtel de Lassay, and the Quai d'Orsay.

Previous pages: A poussoir heads towards the bridge connecting the Cité to the Ile Saint-Louis. On the left, the nave of Notre-Dame with its powerful flying buttresses and the Square de l'Ile-de-France. To the right, the Quai d'Orléans and its aristocratic houses reflected in the water.

the mainland by the Petit-Pont on the Left Bank and the Grand-Pont on the Right Bank. In 1310, the Quai des Orfèvres was built just across from the Right Bank, on what was formerly the Ile de Galilée and was then incorporated into the Ile de la Cité. Downstream, the Ile aux Juifs and the Ile aux Passeurs were not attached to the Cité until 1607 when they became the Place Dauphine. The island called Ile de Louviers has been part of the Right Bank between the Boulevard Morland and the Quai Henri IV since 1843; the Ile Saint-Louis has existed in its present form since Louis XIII. Further to the west, a group of small islands were united during the 15th century, and took the name of Ile Maquerelle, so-called after a species of swan that King Louis XIV used to breed there. Part of the Left Bank since 1773, it runs between Rue Jean-Nicot and Avenue de Suffren, along the Quai d'Orsay and the Quai Branly.

Lutetia – a swamp

On the Right Bank, Lutetia was surrounded by vast marshes with slopes running down towards the shores of the river. Here boats could be moored in preference to the hillier Left Bank where the spur of the Montagne Sainte-Geneviève rose to 70 metres and, during invasions, provided an escape route for the inhabitants. Several small hills and mounds emerged from the swamp and to the west there was a large oak forest, traces of which can still be seen today: the Bois de Boulogne in the Forêt de Rouvray, and also in the forested hills of Chaville, Meudon and Montmorency which used to slope down as far as the Louvre. The heights of the city were the same as they are today: northwards, Montmartre; eastwards, Charonne, Ménilmontant and Belleville; westwards, Chaillot; southwards, the Montagne Sainte-Geneviève.

Two parts of the Paris basin were formed geologically some 600,000 years ago: Chelles (Seine-et-

Marne) and Levallois. In those times, the riverbed of the Seine was much wider than it is today: it went as far north as the present Grands Boulevards and met the present riverbed near the Place de l'Alma. Under the Opéra, there is still a little lake called *Grande-Batelière*, which protects the building from fire, and for a long time hampered the extension of the Galeries Lafayette department store.

On the Left Bank, the river Bièvre played a similar role. It formed a marsh at the point where it met the Seine near the Gare d'Austerlitz. Here also stood one of the many "water stations", as they used to be called, for river passengers. Until the building of the first railway during the Second Empire, it took two and a half days to link Auxerre and Paris by horse-drawn barge. Wine and logs were brought in by the river Yonne to Montereau.

The Parisii and Lutetia

Names such as Rue de la Pierre-Levée, Rue de la Haute-Borne at Ménilmontant, Pierrefitte (pierre fixée) near Saint-Denis all bear witness to megaliths recording prehistoric human activity.

For three centuries before Christ the Celtic population named the Parisii lived in Lutetia, which was already the heart of the Ile-de-France region. They were dominated by their more powerful neighbours, the Senons, who were fishermen, blacksmiths, masons, merchants, boatmen and market-gardeners. Of the natural routes from Rome to the British Isles, one ran through Lyons, Reims and Boulogne, and the other, a very important tin route, along the rivers Garonne and Loire. But Lutetia, an island protected by the Seine and offering a safe stopping place, rapidly established its position. When peace returned, it developed on the Left Bank in the direction of the Arènes, on the eastern slope of the Montagne Sainte-Geneviève.

The Seine, seen from the Pont de Grenelle. At the forefront of the Ile des Cygnes there is a miniature replica of the Statue of Liberty.

The Forum was built in 200 A.D., slightly before the thermal baths at Cluny, a great part of which was destroyed during the Barbarian invasion in 285 when the stones were used to build ramparts round the city. Rough-hewn steps from this period have been found in buildings of the Cité.

During the same period, Lutetia expanded very rapidly. Inland water transport developed, and during the reign of the Roman Emperor Tiberius boatmen built an altar to Jupiter and to the Roman Emperor which was discovered under Notre-Dame… in 1711. Local roads began to intersect the Paris basin, linking Troyes and Rouen and the mouth of the Seine. On the Right Bank, Montmartre was the only populated neighbourhood. Water

was supplied by an aqueduct, running down from the Rungis plateau to the Rue Saint-Jacques.

On our historical tour through Paris, the reader will notice that the same places and roads appear at different periods. We will meet them all along the way, in the labyrinth of the old medieval town as well as in the wide avenues and great vistas of the 19th century.

Paris inside its fortified walls

After the Gallo-Roman period, Paris grew safely inside its fortified walls. As the town expanded, the walls were broken down and rebuilt further out. Lutetia became la Cité and included, under

Philippe-August, the Louvre, the Sorbonne and the Panthéon. Charles V created the districts of Tournelles, Saint-Paul and Bastille, after the revolt of the Maillotins (1383). The ramparts erected by Louis XIII ran from there to what are now the Opéra and the Madeleine. The *Fermiers Généraux* wall, on the eve of the Revolution, ran as far as the Palais de Chaillot (the foot of Montmartre), and behind the Montagne Sainte-Geneviève and the Butte-aux-Cailles (Place d'Italie).

This succession of walls gave protection against the invading Huns, Barbarians, Normans and the English during the Hundred Years' War. But they had an even more important economic and fiscal role: goods entering through the city gates were subject to a variety of taxes, often very unpopular. This in part explains the growth of communes like Charenton and Bercy, where great wine depots were built outside the city limits to house the wine being brought into the area in casks along the river Yonne.

At times accessible to the Provinces and at others shut off from them under the Monarchy, Paris expanded dramatically under Napoleon III, when Baron Haussmann demolished whole districts, built new ones and opened grand vistas which gave light to the city and improved circulation.

years later, the first Parisian "Bureau de Ville' was opened by the *Compagnie du Nord*.

It was, however, principally between the Second Empire and 1875 that the French railway network was developed, from the Grande Ceinture de Paris to the Orient Express, a luxury train of sleeping cars and now the subject of renewed interest.

While the food guides consider the buffet of the Gare de l'Est to have the best table, the Train Bleu restaurant in the Gare de Lyon is famous for its allegorical paintings of 1900.

More recently, development of the T.G.V. (Train à Grande Vitesse) has put the city of Lyons within two and a half hours of Paris.

City Transport

For a long time, horses and mules were the only means of transport. They alone were able to force their way through narrow, jammed streets with open gutters in the middle. In 1550, there were only three private carriages in the capital, but they frightened pedestrians all the same!

Pascal was the creator of the first public transport in 1662: it was very cheap. Sedan-chairs and hackneys had already appeared at the beginning of the 17th century. The horse-drawn omnibus was introduced during the 19th century. During the same period coach stations were widespread, notable examples being in the Rue Bonaparte opposite Saint-Germain-des-Prés and in the Rue Pigalle, where the building was not pulled down till 1969. Then came the trams, the Metro in 1900, and the RER to the Défense in 1970.

Around the city, the Petite Ceinture and Grande Ceinture railways were built in 1875, to link together suburbs and villages on the outskirts.

For centuries, the Seine was the main means of transport for food supplies, commodities and travellers. The horse-drawn barge of Corbeil was so slow that its name was given to carriages in a funeral procession. Nowadays, the charming *bateaux-mouches*, with their open upper-decks, give visitors a unique view of this ever-changing scene of old and new Paris.

Then came the car...

After quiet beginnings in 1890 the motorcar has now gradually taken over the capital. It caused enormous daily traffic jams when offices shut, despite the roads created along the banks of the Seine and the Boulevard Périphérique which were designed to give direct access to outlying suburbs and to prevent too much congestion in the centre of the city.

The canal Saint-Martin starts at the Villette Lock (19ᵉ) and meets the Seine at the Pont d'Austerlitz, on the Right Bank. Its important commercial traffic includes a new "patache eautobus", a mini-barge with seating for 55 pasengers.

Communications

Transport changed more in the 19th century than it had since the invention of the wheel. Pilgrims used to walk 20 kilometres a day on the way to Rome or to Santiago de Compostella; a horseman could cover 6 kilometres an hour, a stage-coach a little less. The teams of oxen bringing casks of Burgundy to the capital covered 12 kilometres a day, as evidenced by the old staging posts.

The revolution which began in England in 1825 with the advent of the railway, was to change the way of life and the transport systems of the entire world. In 1837, Queen Marie-Amélie inaugurated the first passenger line in France: Paris-Saint-Germain-en-Laye (18 kilometres), its departure point a wooden hut, now the Gare Saint-Lazare, the third most important station in France. Ten

Aeroplanes and airports

The *montgolfière*, a type of balloon, was invented 200 years ago in France. It is now forbidden to fly hot-air balloons over Paris, although their round, colourful shapes can still be seen in the sky over the Ile-de-France region.

Santos-Dumont was a very prolific inventor in the field of aerial navigation. He lived on the Champs-Elysées at the beginning of this century and used to anchor his airship to the balcony of his dining-room!

The first airport was built at Le Bourget, to the north of the city. Charles Lindberg landed there on 21 May, 1927 after flying the Atlantic. Parisians came in their thousands to cheer his achievement. After the Second World War, Orly was built, and more recently, at Roissy-en-France, the Charles-de-Gaulle airport was constructed, with two parallel runways. An express link joins the Gare du Nord to the Charles-de-Gaulle airport, putting New York within three hours of central Paris by direct flight on Concorde.

The Issy-les-Moulineaux heliport is alongside the Boulevard Périphérique downstream from the Auteuil bridge.

The Gare du Nord with its immense glass wall, a "functional" palace of imperial Paris. It forms part of the vista, seen from the Place de la République, of the Boulevard Magenta, one of the great avenues created by Baron Haussmann.

OLD PARIS AND THE LATIN QUARTER

The Middle Ages

When the Roman Empire collapsed, a new universal institution took its place: Christendom. The Popes, whose temporal powers were very limited, sought to establish a political balance in Europe. The first step was an alliance with the Franks. The title of "Emperor" was reinstated and given to Charlemagne who established his throne in Aix-la-Chapelle and created schools there. The weakness of his successors led to the break-up of Europe, which disintegrated into a feudal system and serfdom. Islam, on the other hand, expanded rapidly. In the 7th century A.D. it spread from the borders of India to the Atlantic, serving as an intermediary between the Far East and the West, introducing paper, wood engraving, printing and Arabic numerals to Europe.

The Foundation of the Church of France

A few dates
451: Saint Geneviève, by her prayers, saved Paris from Attila's Huns and became its patron saint.
910: The Cluny Abbey was founded in Burgundy. Its priests played a principal part in creating the Latin Quarter in Paris.

L'Ile de la Cité

In the 8th century, on the Ile de la Cité, near the narrow arm of the Seine, Notre-Dame stood on a

Stained glass windows of Notre-Dame: only the three large rose-windows have kept part of the 13th century originals. The window on the west side of the facade represents traditional monthly activities and signs of the Zodiac around the Virgin Mary. The northern window features the Patriarchs, the Kings of the Old Testament, and also has the Virgin Mary at its centre; the southern rose-window represents the Wise and the Foolish Virgins, the Martyrs, the Confessors, and the Apostles surrounding Christ.

Left: Notre-Dame's facade behind the Petit-Pont.

square surrounded by shops, by the Bishop's palace, a cloister with canons' houses, and a charity hospital which was later to become the Hôtel-Dieu. The writer Grégoire de Tours mentions the existence of five churches in the area at this time.

Saint Germain was buried in the Saint-Vincent basilica and gave his name to it, and there are still several small columns from the original Merovingian building in Saint-Germain-des-Prés. The original basilica had been designed in the ancient Greek architectural style of the Acropolis temples.

Nearer to the Seine, a church was dedicated to Saint Julian. The sacred relics of Saint Geneviève were moved and buried in the Basilique des Saints-Apôtres which eventually took her name. Her reliquary was carried at the head of religious processions whenever the capital was threatened. When the Normans attacked the city, people from the outlying districts took refuge in the Ile de la Cité, carrying with them the sacred relics of their local saints; and the places where they left those relics became holy sites for new churches. Later the great religious orders, by building churches, created the places where people would live and a church surrounded by a cluster of houses is still one of the distinguishing features of many French villages.

Water-mills in the 11th Century

In the 11th century once again Western Europe experienced rapid development. Great technical improvements took place especially in agriculture, one of the decisive inventions being the water-mill. In time, most bridges around Paris had their own water-mills, the most famous being at Charenton on the river Marne.

On the Left Bank the centres of growth were at the end of the Petit Pont, which linked it to the Cité: the site of the bridge has remained unchanged from since before the Roman conquest. A bishop of the 9th century gave his name to the *Bourg Saint–Marcel*, built around his chapel, and located between the Salpêtrière and what is today the Rue Descartes. *Saint-Germain-des-Prés* was already a famous spot. The tomb of the saint, who was reputed to have performed many miracles, attracted many visitors and brought the abbey great importance and wealth so that it eventually became independent of the Episcopate. It owned most of the islands on the Seine, all the way down to Billancourt. It brought fame and fortune to the Left Bank and put its stamp on the whole Latin Quarter. The *Porte Saint-Michel* is located at the intersection of the Rue Monsieur-le-Prince and the Boulevard Saint-Michel, the famous Boul-'Mich'.

Philippe-Auguste gives shape to the capital of France

King Philippe-Auguste gave an important impetus to the fortified capital's development by building walls to protect Paris and its 190,000 inhabitants

Left: The Seine at Notre-Dame, one of the most beautiful views of Paris beloved of painters and photographers. In the foreground, the Pont de l'Archevêché. The spire, restored by Viollet-le-Duc, is 45 metres high. The Cathedral rests upon flying buttresses 15 metres high.

from English invaders. His walls took in most of the inhabited centre of the city, including its gardens, meadows, vineyards and paddocks, with a view to future development, and lasted almost 150 years. Each new wall lengthened the perimeter without destroying the network of streets and alleys, many traces of which remain, although they have been incorporated in successive rebuilding.

But the King looked far ahead on behalf of posterity. Clever and obstinate, he resumed the struggle against the English Plantagenets and, at Bouvines, won the battle which assured the future of the French monarchy. It also led to the political decline of the Holy Roman Empire, the end of English domination north of the Loire, and eventually to the weakening of royal power in England where the feudal barons imposed the Magna Carta upon King John.

In France, administrative power shifted into the hands of baliffs and Seneschals, officers of the King.

The University trained burghers, administrators and judges all of whom belonged to the King's court. The urban bourgeoisie (especially Parisian) received privileges and in return actively supported the Monarchy. Philippe-Auguste divided the capital into three areas. He centralized and concentrated the administration between the Cité and the Louvre, which he began

to build and which his successors made a point of enlarging and improving in accordance with contemporary taste.

His reign marked the evolution of the deeply religious Romanesque architecture seen in the abbeys of Cluny, Vezelay and Autun, towards the Gothic style. This was also the period when chivalry developed both as a code and a way of life with its corollary, courtly love, of which the troubadours were the bards.

The Cité was then a huge building site between the Palais Royal and Notre-Dame. On the island there were some thirty narrow, muddy, stinking streets, cleaned only by the floods. The smells were so bad that the King ordered the provost of the merchants to pave the streets nearest to the Louvre. Some of these original paving stones can still be seen in the garden of the Musée de Cluny, whose medieval exhibits are among the finest in the capital.

Watermen and bridges

The commercial quarters of the city developed on the Right Bank around the Hôtel de Ville. The prosperity of Paris depended on its ports along the Seine, where many merchants and boatmen settled because the gentle slopes allowed easy mooring for their boats. Each guild had its own

From Notre-Dame's tower, a gargoyle representing a devil looks down on the labyrinth of streets and monuments, so well described by the 19th century writer Victor Hugo. The taller houses on the left have been resurfaced with the characteristic white Montmartre plaster.

Stained glass windows in the Sainte-Chapelle. It was built, in a very short time, by Saint Louis to contain the relics of Christ's Passion. Concerts of sacred music given here have a devoted following.

Right: The Tour Saint-Jacques, bell-tower of the Eglise Saint-Jacques-de-la-Boucherie, located at the beginning of the Rue de Rivoli, is one of the most ancient sites of Paris. Built in the Flamboyant Gothic style, it was completely restored under the Second Empire.

banks of the city before the Gallic War. The Gallic chief Calumogène had them destroyed in an attempt to protect Lutetia from Labienus' legions (Labienus was Caesar's lieutenant). When they were rebuilt, they were called the *Grand Pont* and the *Petit Pont*. The Grand Pont stretched across the northern arm of the Cité (it is impossible today to locate the precise spot, but it was probably the Pont-au-Change or the Pont Notre-Dame). The Petit Pont connected the island to the Left Bank, thus linking the Cité to the Roman roads to Lyons and Orleans, to the abbeys of Saint-Germain-des-Prés and Saint-Victor, and to the University.

On these bridges, as on those built later between the 12th and 18th centuries, stood wooden houses like the silversmith stalls one can still admire today on the *Ponte Vecchio* in Florence.

Teachers and students in the Latin Quarter

Philippe-Auguste's most outstanding contribution was in the intellectual sphere. On the Left Bank he gathered together some 12,000 boys and teachers from various parishes and created what later became the *petites écoles*, where children learned to read, write, count, say their catechism and sing. The Church was given the sole authority to educate, under the aegis of the bishops. Instructions were given by the Pope and every abbey, priory and parish taught in Latin – hence the name Latin Quarter for the new district. Indeed, Latin remained the common written language throughout Europe for several centuries – until, in fact, it was replaced by French at the diplomatic and cultural levels.

The school of the *Cloître Notre-Dame* was a small cultural city in itself, the birthplace of the University. The seven sciences known at the time were taught at the highest level, and a king's son, cardinals' nephews, even a pope came to learn, attracted by the reputation of such illustrious teachers as Abélard, Guillaume de Champeaux and Maurice de Sully (the designer of Notre-Dame), among many others. Teachers and students were scholars and wore their hair tonsured. In the beginning they used to gather round the Eglise Saint-Julien-le-Pauvre, which was situated at one of the most important crossroads of the capital. There, since the 6th century, had been a chapel dedicated to Saint Julian the Hospitaller, which included a hostel for the many pilgrims and travellers who journeyed through Europe on foot. A victim of the Norman invasion, the church was rebuilt in the 12th century by the Benedictines from Longpont in a style foreshadowing the Gothic. It is today the oldest church in Paris. Saint Thomas Aquinas, Dante, Petrarch and, later, Rabelais and Villon all came to pray in the church. In the nearby square, stands a false acacia, planted in 1601 and supposed to be the oldest tree in the city. Those early lessons were given out of doors, in the Rue du Fouarre and Place Maubert, the teacher standing on a platform and the students

port, the grain port being close to what later became the Place de Grève. The port for tiles was near the Hôtel-Dieu, while the more valuable stone and marble were stored further west. The port for hay, situated near the site of the present Pont-Neuf, played a very important role in providing fodder for the countless animals which fed and transported the ever-growing population of Paris. The watermen's guild, very powerful since the days of Lutetia, was given a monopoly for selling water and carrying commodities and goods between the bridges of Mantes and Paris. And when the municipal administration was entrusted to them, these merchants modelled it on their own guild organizations.

There were two wooden bridges linking the two

The pepper pot towers of the Conciergerie remain a powerful symbol of the medieval Palais-Royal, erected around 1300. They were restored in the 19th century at the same time as the Palais de Justice. Under the Terror, the arcade on the right wing was the entrance to the jail where Queen Marie-Antoinette was imprisoned before her execution.

sitting on the ground or on bales of hay.

It was here that the Rector of the University was elected.

From the 12th century on, the intellectual life of Europe began to concentrate on Paris. Teachers and students came from all over the continent, attracted by its theological, philosophical and political teachings.

In 1253, Robert de Sorbon, the chaplain of Saint-Louis, created the *Sorbonne*. The University was complemented by colleges which started out as student hostels providing bed and board. The first one was founded in 1180 by an Englishman, Josse de Londres. Later, every abbey had its own college with a chapel (some of them can still be visited). They were located between the Saint-Victor Abbey (*faculté de Jussieu*) and the Place du Panthéon. One of the most famous colleges, *Saint-Barbe*, had as students Ignatius Loyola and Francis-Xavier, the founders of the Jesuit order.

This cultural city developed on the Montagne Sainte-Geneviève. *Saint-Etienne-du-Mont* became its main church in the 15th century.

Saint Louis and the Sainte-Chapelle

Saint Louis, grandson of Philippe-Auguste, enhanced the importance of spiritual and daily life in Paris, increasing the power and prestige of the monarchy. The King reinforced the authority of Royal Justice by dispensing it himself, directly, under an oak tree in the Bois de Vincennes, a forest in which he loved to live and hunt.

Saint Louis' greatest architectural achievement was the *Sainte-Chapelle* which he had built to contain the relics of Chirst's Passion: a fragment of the True Cross, the Sponge, the Spear and the Crown of Thorns bought from the Emperor Baudouin of Constantinople. The Sainte-Chapelle was built in a very short time, in the new Gothic style: the intersecting ribs of its vaulting supported by flying buttresses give it a remarkable brightness and lightness, and enhance its proportions. Its beauty became a model for architecture throughout the Ile-de-France region and inspired many churches around which villages and towns were built, especially in the department of the Oise.

The new techniques that had been applied to the

Sainte-Chapelle were developed further in the 12th century: for example, statues in the form of columns were replaced by figures in a more flowing style. It was an urban art, the reverse of the rural Romanesque style, which encouraged an enthusiastic competitive spirit between towns.

The King's Court

By the beginning of the 14th century royal power was firmly established. Philippe-le-Bel embellished the Palais Royal in the Ile de la Cité. He added a new wing to the Petit Palais, comprising the famous Gothic rooms, extended later by the Conciergerie. The King's court was established there, and at first it was called the Royal Council: as early as 1250, it was holding judicial sessions and later became the Parliament of the land. From then on, the important decisions concerning the Kingdom were taken in Paris.

In the 13th century daily life in the capital was notable for the multiplicity of its trades, each regulated by a guild. These skilled trades made possible a great flowering of all the arts supported by royal and noble patronage.

The Gothic style in architecture was paralleled in

Above: The Tour de l'Horloge: on the right side of the facade is the first Parisian public clock. It was made under Henri III, in a polychromic style. At the top is the King's monogram, and around are symbolic sculptures.

The booksellers' stalls on the quais of the Seine offer old and new books, and prints. Originally, they sold various items that had been fished out of the Seine.

sculpture and in painting, and the work of the illuminators was of such fine quality that Dante refers to them in his writings. The most perfect example which has come down to us, *Les Très Riches Heures du duc de Berry*, was produced for this princely patron by famous painters of the 15th century. The book is illustrated with delightful little tableaux depicting the activities of the humble and the great alike, and is one of the great masterpieces of the Musée de Chantilly (Oise).

Charles V

During the disturbances that foreshadowed the Hundred Years' War, which ruined the country and killed one-third of its population, Charles V had realized that the Cité was vulnerable. So at the other other end of Paris he built the districts of *Saint-Antoine* and *Saint-Paul*, and a vast palace for himself in Vincennes. He enlarged the fortified walls built by Philippe-Auguste on the Right Bank; and for this it was necessary at various times to demolish or enlarge neighbourhoods. A moat was dug and filled with water, and the rubble was used to build a parapet protected by walls and square towers, with a ditch on the country side.

On the Left Bank, the *Petit Châtelet* was rebuilt; its new gates were moved further out to accommodate the city, which had expanded to 439 hectares. Charles V, a great builder, developed the Right Bank and made it safer than the Cité from which he had been forced to flee during the revolt organized by Etienne Marcel, provost of the merchants. To this King we owe the *Couvent des Célestins* and the *Pont Saint-Michel*. He made his residence in the fortress of the Louvre and, in 1368, he installed his library there – the forerunner of the Bibliothèque Nationale – his ceremonial rooms, his collections and his baths. He also built a magnificent staircase.

The Brasserie Lipp, at Saint-Germain-des-Prés. Famous since the 12th century it still attracts visitors and locals, and is a popular meeting place for politicians, journalists and writers. It is particularly known for its sauerkraut and Baltic herrings.

Left: The Rue de Rennes, seen from the Tour Montparnasse, one of the highest points in the capital. It runs down to Saint-Germain-des-Prés. Behind the church tower is the dome of the Institut de France opposite the Louvre. Beyond is the Eglise Saint-Eustache, revealed by the demolition of Les Halles, and the Samaritaine department store. To the right, the Eglise Saint-Sulpice.

The Sorbonne: founded by Robert de Sorbon, Chaplain to Saint Louis. Protected by Richelieu, it was rebuilt in 1627. Its church was the first in Paris to have a cupola in the 17th century.

Right: Rue Mouffetard (5ᵉ), one of the most picturesque markets in Paris. Some of the houses date from the 16th century. Here, around the Eglise Saint-Médard, and in the Rue de Buci (6ᵉ), are to be found the best examples of architecture in the working class districts of the time.

ROYAL PARIS

A Time of Crisis

The 13th century had been a time of steady progress and of relative harmony, but the 14th and 15th centuries witnessed many crises: the Hundred Years' War devastated the land; famine and plague reduced the French population by one-third and caused social unrest in villages and towns alike; and crisis within the Church had far-reaching consequences at all levels of society. All these calamities slowed down France's progress in comparison with its neighbours. The Holy Roman Empire recovered slowly. Attacked by the English, the Armagnacs and the rapidly expanding Burgundians, France shrank to a small area which was later defended by Joan of Arc and her people's army. During the same period, a decisive technical revolution was taking place: Johannes Gutenberg of Mainz invented the printing press, inspired in part by the wine press, and the first printed book to reach France was the Bible in 1470.

Discovery of America by Christopher Columbus

Progress was further stimulated by the improvements in map making and the techniques of navigation, including the compass brought back from China by Marco Polo, and the newly designed sailing ship. All these were to aid in the discovery of America by Christopher Columbus in 1492. The Genoese navigator, sailing in the service of Isabella of Castille, thought he had

Above: Joan of Arc's gilded bronze statue in the Place des Pyramides, raised in honour of the heroine who tried to recapture Paris from the English during the Hundred Years' War. Religious and patriotic processions take place every year on 8 May, her feast day.

Left: the Château de Vincennes: built by Charles V, it is a huge rectangle 320 by 178 metres, enclosed by a thick wall and a continuous moat. The massive keep dominates the west front.

found the route to India and its legendary riches when he landed at Guanahani (San Salvador). The new continent was named America in 1507 after the Italian navigator, Amerigo Vespucci.

These discoveries gave Europe a new dimension. Made largely by Spanish and Portuguese explorers (or by explorers of other nations in the service of the Spanish and Portuguese monarchs) they brought the Iberian Peninsula great prestige and influence, and much valuable metal. Between 1500 and 1650, 200,000 kilograms of gold and 17,000,000 kilograms of silver were shipped into the Peninsula from the New World, giving a powerful economic stimulus from which all Europe benefited.

Of particular interest to Parisians, was the exploration and opening up of Canada in 1534 by the Frenchman Jacques Cartier.

In the arts, the Italian Renaissance was in full flower, and the best painters, sculptors and goldsmiths of that country were invited to France by François I.

Louis XI and the Royal House of Tournelles

The Right Bank of the Seine, at first left to merchants and boatmen, was developed as the marshes were gradually drained. Just before the Hundred Years' War Charles V built the *Saint-Paul* and *Saint-Antoine* districts.

At this time the Seine had a second crescent-shaped arm, that flowed between the present Boulevards du Temple and Beaumarchais on one

Henri IV's statue, opposite the Place Dauphine and the Palais de Justice. A very popular King, he became famous for his slogan: A chicken in every pot on Sundays.

side, and the Pont de l'Alma on the other: it was this enormous swamp which was later drained to become Le Marais.

The *Royal House of Tournelles* owes its name to its numerous towers. Its out-buildings and gardens extended between the boulevard and the streets now called Saint-Antoine, Saint-Claude and Turenne. It was originally conceived as the Hôtel Saint-Pol and included several residences, chapels, bath-houses, servants quarters, cloisters and inner courtyards, two parks, six gardens, small woods, menageries, a maze and meadows. From it derive the names of the present Rue des Foins (Hay Street) and Rue Beautreillis (which recalls a royal vineyard).

Louis XI lived there, Louis XII died there, as did

Henri II from a head wound received in a tournament held to mark the marriage of his sister Marguerite to Duke Philibert-Emmanuel of Savoy. His widow, Catherine de Medici, went to live at the Louvre, and ordered the demolition of the building in 1563.

Saint-Germain l'Auxerrois, Parish Church of Kings

The church of *Saint-Germain-l'Auxerrois* was dedicated to the Bishop of Auxerre, the spiritual father of Saint Geneviève. Rebuilt three times, it acquired great importance when it became the royal parish church. Vestiges of the Romanesque

(the original building) can still be seen today; the choir and the portal are Gothic, while the porch, nave and transept are Flamboyant Gothic.
In 1472 at the Sorbonne the first Parisian printing house was established in the Rue Sain=-Jacques.

Popular festivities and celebrations

Festivities and sporting events such as tournaments, which anyone could attend, were part of medieval daily life. The Carrousel, a display of horsemanship both less warlike and more aristocratic, tended to replace tournaments after the death of Henri II. Tennis (*jeu de paume*) was at first played with bare hands, and then, from the beginning of the 15th century, with a racket. This is *real* tennis played outdoors and without a net.

François I, a capricious ruler...

During the Hundred Years' War and after, Paris was neglected by its Kings who much preferred to live in Vincennes or in the Loire valley. François I strengthened the links between the capital and the monarchy, ruling according to his whim in spite of severe financial difficulties. He founded the Collège Royal (now the Collège de France) to provide free instruction in Latin, Greek and Hebrew. The Notre-Dame bridge connecting the Cité

The Hôtel des Archevêques de Sens in the Rue de Figuier (4ᵉ), its turrets capped by pepperpot roofs; one of the oldest buildings in the capital, it was built at the end of the 15th century. It is now the Forney Library belonging to the City of Paris.

Following pages: The Institut de France seen from the Quai du Louvre, and the Footbridge of the Pont des Arts: one of the finest views of the capital. It was originally the Collège des Quatre-Nations, built towards the end of the 17th century to meet the wishes of Cardinal Mazarin, once buried under the cupola.

Left: The origin of the Quartier du Marais: the Place Royale (now Place des Vosges), located in the 3ᵉ and 4ᵉ. It was Henri IV's great architectural achievement, built on the site of the Tournelles, a former Royal medieval residence. The principal houses in the square soon became very fashionable; they are listed buildings now.

Opposite: A fountain in the garden of the Place des Vosges where, on the occasion of the marriage of Louis XIII to Anne of Austria, 1300 horsemen performed before an audience of 10,000.

Below: Under the shade of the arcades of the Place des Vosges, several cafés and restaurants welcome tourists. Victor Hugo lived here from 1832 to 1848 in a house that has since become a Museum.

to the Right Bank collapsed with its sixty-five houses in 1499 and took ten years to rebuild: it had six arches, carried sixty-eight numbered houses and was guarded at each corner by identical turrets. The houses were made of brick reinforced by stonework and with gables overlooking the roadway, and there were arcades of shops at ground level. When completed, the bridge was no longer at the same level as the Rue de la Cité into which it ran, and it became necessary to raise that street and rebuild all its houses to the same height and design.

After Francois I's defeat at Pavia and his captivity in Madrid, he came to an understanding with the Parisian bourgeoisie, who had contributed substantially to the ransom which obtained his freedom, and he took up residence in the capital. In 1519, he bought a property for his mother, Louise de Savoie, in the *Faubourg Saint-Honoré*, a district of many tileworks.

He also began improving the Louvre. In 1528 the keep was demolished and the main entrance-gate overlooking the Seine was closed. The path that ran alongside the river was replaced by a 40-metre long embankment between the Châtelet and the

ramparts, thus forming a direct link between the Louvre and the Palais. Beyond the fortified walls, the road continued towards Boulogne, where the King ordered the building of the Résidence de Madrid. The *Porte* Neuve was built, opening on to the site of the present Pont Royal. The main entrance was moved to the east side, looking towards Saint-Germain-l'Auxerrois and the King ordered a road, the Rue d'Autriche, to be cut in the same direction.

Lescot's 1546 plant for the Louvre provided for two residences: one, on the east, was the original fortress which was to be refurbished, and one, on the west, was to be laid out in the Tuileries, and had a series of covered galleries linking it with a garden to the west of the Tuileries. The project, spread over three centuries, was finally completed by Napoleon III, and partly destroyed by the Commune.

François I also gave his strong support to the Classic style of architecture which was soon to flourish as whole new districts were developed in and around the capital.

The Pont-Neuf

The Faubourg Saint-Germain soon became an important district lined by fine mansions. The inhabitants demanded a new bridge, and Henri III laid the first stone of the Pont-Neuf in 1578. The abbot's palace at Saint-Germain-des-Prés dates from the same period; its facade of bricks reinforced by stonework contrasts with its slate roofs.

The Wars of Religion slowed down the growth of Paris. In 1603 Henri IV crossed the Pont-Neuf on horseback. At the second arch the King had a pump installed to bring water to the Louvre and the Tuileries. The water tower consisted of a room decorated with a bas relief showing the woman of Samaria pouring water for Christ. In this working-class district where actors performed in the streets, the water tower and its clock with automata were one of the sights of Paris. The Pont-Neuf was the first bridge that directly connected the two banks of the Seine. In the middle it rested on the tip of the Ile de la Cité, which had been enlarged by the small islands making up the Place Dauphine.

The Place Royale

Henri IV's great achievement on the Right Bank was the Place Royale, on the site of the Tournelles. With the object of combining the useful with the pleasing, he wanted to establish new silk factories in the square, and at the same time provide a place where Parisians could walk and admire the houses built of brick and stone with their arcades of shops. The Place Royale was inaugurated on the occasion of the marriage of Louis XIII and Anne of Austria. During the Revolution it was renamed Place des Vosges.

On what was formerly a marsh (and is still called the Marais), a whole new fashionable quarter was built, which was quickly taken over by the aristocracy with their splendid mansions. Jean

Androuet du Cerceau built and decorated the Hôtel de Sully in the present Rue Saint-Antoine. The Hôtel Carnavalet, a marvel of classical Renaissance style and the work of Pierre Lescot and Jean Goujon, was occupied by Madame de Sévigné in the 17th century. Now the Musée Historique de la Ville de Paris, it houses a collection of views and plans of Paris from the 16th century to the present day, and sets of magnificent costumes.

In the Rue du Figuier, at the corner of the Rue de la Fauconnerie (4ᵉ) is the extraordinary *Hôtel des Archevêques de Sens* dating from 1475 and built in Flamboyant Gothic style. It was remodelled and restored in the 17th century and is now occupied by the Bibliothèque Forney. Nearby is the former Hôtel Guénégaud which houses the Maison de la Chasse et de la Nature.

After Henri IV's assassination in 1610, his widow Marie de Medici built the Palais du Luxembourg and decorated it with paintings by Rubens, which can now be seen in the Louvre. Also on the Left Bank, Jean Hérouard, botanist and Louis XII's principal physician, urged the creation of a royal garden of medicinal herbs. That garden was the forerunner of the Jardin des Plantes, which today owns almost 15,000 plant species, a library of 250,000 books and some very rare trees.

Ile Saint-Louis

Among the great works planned by Henri IV, was the creation of a fine quarter based on two small islands upstream from the Place de Grève; the Ile aux Vaches and the Ile Notre-Dame. This plan was carried out with happy results by his son Louis XIII and by his widow Marie de Medici. The work lasted thirty years: from the start the Ile Nôtre-Dame (renamed the Ile Saint-Louis in the 18th century) became an extension of the Marais by virtue of its luxurious and beautiful mansions built by Louis and François Le Vau for important officials and financiers. It has remained unchanged and timeless, a charming corner of the 17th century.

The Palais Cardinal

Cardinal Richelieu became Louis XIII's minister in 1624 and he instructed the architect Lemercier to build him a mansion on a site near the Louvre, between the present Rue de Valois and Rue de Richelieu, which he extended by taking in the land adjoining the wall built by Charles V.

In 1635 Richelieu founded the Académie Francaise which was given the specific task of compiling a dictionary of the French language. Today it comprises forty members, the Immortals, elected for life. The induction of new members, a fashionable literary event, is held under the dome of the old church facing the Palais du Louvre and built originally to receive Cardinal Mazarin's mortal remains.

Louis XIII inherited the Palais Cardinal from Richelieu and his widow went to live there with her two sons in 1643. The name of the palace was then changed to the Palais-Royal. It was from here during the Fronde in January 1650 that the royal

The Ile Saint-Louis, upstream from the Place de Grève (Hôtel-de-Ville). Surrounded by its quais, it offers a perfect example of classical 17th century architecture between the Pont-Marie and the Pont de Sully – a step outside time.

Opposite: Details of columns, ornaments and terraces with balustrades adorned with ornamental vases, repeated over sixty pavilions, opening on to gardens with lawns and stretches of water.

Below: The Palais Royal was built near the Louvre for Cardinal Richelieu, minister to Louis XIII. After a fire in 1765, the palace was rebuilt in its present form, with a number of gaming houses above an arcade of shops.

family was forced to flee to Saint-Germain-en-Laye. When the troubles were over, the queen preferred to return to the shelter of the Louvre. Later, the Orleans Branch of the monarchy took over and occupied the Palais-Royal. *Monsieur*, the King's brother, restored it, embellished it, and gave many fine parties there; and he opened the gardens to the public. His descendants altered the palace considerably. The gardens provided a favourite Parisian walk until the time of the Empire.

Luxurious mansions sprang up around the Louvre as did gardens. On the Right Bank the most famous garden was the *Cours-la-Reine*, designed for Marie de Medici at the new Porte de la Conférence, and linking the villages of Chaillot, Bas-Roule and Ville-l'Evêque with Paris. It was planted with four rows of elms, bounded by ditches and closed by a gate at each end. It was a forerunner of the Champs-Elysées.

Anne of Austria and the Great Monasteries

The Counter Reformation created new religious orders, monasteries and convents; it also reformed old ones and established seminaries. *Saint-Nicolas-du-Chardonnet* was founded in 1612, *Saint-Sulpice* in 1645. In 1625, the Cistercian nuns of *Port-Royal* moved to the Left Bank. Here was to be one of the main centres of Jansenism which was to play an important part in French thought in the 17th century. The chapel and several buildings can still be seen in the Baudelocque maternity hospital.

Anne of Austria's great achievement was the Benedictine abbey of *Val-de-Grâce*. After Louis XIV's birth, she transformed the monastery, which continued to be improved and added to until the Revolution. In 1795 the buildings became a military hospital.

Mazarin and the Bibliothèque Nationale

After the *Fronde* was subdued, Cardinal Mazarin came to live near the Palais-Royal, in the *Hôtel Tubeuf*, which was to become part of the *Bibliothèque Nationale*. Today it contains 6 million printed books, just about as many engravings, 136,000 manuscripts and more than 400,000 medals and coins.

Cardinal Mazarin died in 1661, leaving a considerable fortune, including a legacy for building a college, a riding school and a library open to the public twice a week. This group of buildings, now the Bibliothèque Mazarine and the Institut, was built by the architect Le Vau on the site of the gateway and Nesle Tower.

The Mazarine Library has kept its original 18th century decoration, with its old wooden panelling polished by time, and its green curtains. Its volumes include 50,000 books which belonged to convents and victims of the Revolution. Some once belonged to the royal family.

THE GREAT BUILDINGS OF THE OLD REGIME

When Louis XIV became King of France in 1661, Europe was beset by political and social struggles, especially in France, Holland and England. The German States were severely weakened by the Thirty Years' War which devastated their territories and brought to an end the Habsbourg hegemony which Louis XIV would successfully supplant.

Louis XIV at Versailles

The humiliating memories of the Fronde led the King to choose to live far from unruly Paris. He transformed the Hunting Lodge at Versailles into an extraordinary palace, imitated throughout the whole of Europe. Le Vau, Mansart and Hardouin-Mansart were his architects, and Colbert was the superintendent of his buildings.

Paris, however, was not forgotten. A lieutenant of police, Nicolas de la Reynie, was put in charge of public safety, hygiene and lighting, and he regulated the use of shop signs and controlled journalists, story writers and lampoonists. Posters had already begun to appear at the beginning of the century. In 1631 Theophraste Renaudot published the first newspaper *La Gazette de France*, which survived until the First World War.

Colbert, the King's most important minister, had trees planted along the City walls and created vistas ending in triumphal arches celebrating military victories that were achieved later by...Napoleon!

Above:An equestrian statue of Louis XIV in the Place des Victoires. The square is circular in shape, made of white wrought stone, to the design of J H Mansart. The mansions have uniform facades of two stories built over tall arcades with semicircular arches embellished by sculpted heads and pilasters.

Left:Part of the dome of one of the Louvre's pavilions: a Renaissance pastiche with caryatids and statues, built during the reign of Napoleon III. It is located in the main courtyard just in front of the gates on to the Rue de Rivoli.

The Invalides in the Plaine de Grenelle

In the middle of the 17th century, the Plaine de Grenelle was a small warren, a hunting ground where aristocrats used to hunt hares and quails. This was the setting for the Hôtel Royal des Invalides, begun in 1670 to house soldiers disabled in the service of the King. It was built on a site between the Faubourg Saint-Germain and the hamlet of Gros-Caillou near the Pont de l'Alma. Nearly 6000 soldiers were housed there in 1706. The Hôtel was the work of Libéral Bruand and, from 1677, of Jules Hardouin-Mansart who finished the church and built its dome. The whole building has kept its 17th century appearance; part of it now houses the Musée de l'Armée.

The Hôtel des Invalides shared its chancel and altar with the *Eglise du Dôme* until the crypt was built in the centre of the church in 1842. The two buildings are now separated by a marble, multi-coloured portico topped by a large window. The dome of the church rises 107 metres into the Paris sky. Today the subsidiary buildings have been demolished and the superintendent's garden has been replanted near the Place Vauban. The Hôtel des Invalides took five years to be completed. Its architectural style is known in France as "Jesuit" after the Jesuits' first church in Rome. Napoleon's coffin was transferred to the Invalides in 1840 and his monument was built in the crypt in 1861.

The Ecole Militaire (7ᵉ), west
of the Hôtel des Invalides. Designed by Jacques Ange Gabriel, during the reign of Louis
XV, it is an imposing building. Its facade, overlooking
the Champ-de-Mars, was
completed in 1770. It in-
cludes a central pavilion
with Corinthian columns.

Previous pages: The
monumental facade of the Invalides created by Louis XIV
to house his disabled soldiers. In the background the
Eglise du Dôme, with Napoleon's Tomb.

Le Nôtre and the Tuileries Gardens

In the Louvre, Le Brun created the *Galerie d'Apol-
lon*, Le Vau and d'Orbay built the *Pavillon de
Marsan* at the Tuileries and Le Nôtre redesigned
the garden. In so doing, he helped create the
formal sculpted gardens, which became so popular throughout Europe at the time.

The Faubourg Saint-Honoré grew and was embellished. Following Louvois' advice, the King
bought the *Hôtel de Vendôme* and constructed a
large square with octagonal facades: now *Place
Vendôme*.

The Place des Victoires

From 1700 a whole new city grew in this district,
now the Boulevard des Italiens. Between it and
the old town lay the palaces of Cardinals Richelieu and Mazarin and, on the other side of the
present Rue Vivienne, the Hôtel Colbert with its
outbuildings and gardens. After the peace of
Nimegen Marshal de la Feuillade laid out the
Place des Victoires. Built to the design of Mansart,
it was circular, in white stone, with a statue of the
king on foot in the centre.

Water had always been scarce in Paris (there were
no underground sewers until the Second Empire).
In 1670, two hydraulic pumps were installed at the
Pont Notre-Dame in order to raise the level of the
Seine and to supply forty public fountains. Street
lighting and fire fighting services were improved.
Louis XIV authorized a public coach service – *le
carrosse à cinq soles* – invented by the philos-
opher Pascal, which had five routes across Paris.
Street life concentrated around the Pont-Neuf,
where secondhand booksellers, mountebanks
and authors collected to sell their wares.

Theatre was at its zenith. Molière's company settled first at the Palais-Royal, in the Rue Mazarine.
It incorporated a couple of other companies: the
Troupe du Théâtre du Marais which gave the first
performances of most of Corneille's plays, and
from 1680 the Troupe de l'Hotel de Bourgogne
which staged Racine's tragedies, from *Androma-
que* on. The fusion of these three companies resulted in the creation of the *Troupe des Comédiens
du Roi* later the *Comédie-Française*.

The *Académie Royale de Musique* was founded in
1661 and gave its first public concert in 1671.

The manufacture of glass was established in 1665
by craftsmen from Murano, near Venice. In 1667
the Gobelins dyeworks became the royal factory
for furniture and tapestries.

The Fontaine des Innocents (1^e), located in the square that bears the same name, was erected on the site of the cemetery and church of the Saints-Innocents, the most important Parisian necropolis outside the city limits on the road leading to Saint-Denis.

The Hôtel de Ville: burnt down during the Commune, the present building was rebuilt and enlarged fourfold. It is in the Renaissance style, to plans by Boccador. At sunset the light in the public rooms overlooking the Seine presents a unique spectacle.

The Regency and the Parisian Bourgeoisie

After the King's death, the Regent Philippe d'Orleans was forced to seek the support of the Paris bourgeoisie. This happened when the city was ruined by the collapse of Law's system, which was based on speculation. In fact, although many families were affected, the return of the Court to Paris, new fortunes and the role played by financiers resulted in a building boom around the Louvre and in the neighbouring districts. Beyond the Porte Saint-Honoré, Mollet built a mansion that was to become very famous. It belonged first to Madame de Pompadour then, during the Empire, Josephine, Napoleon, Alexander I of Russia and George Washington all lived there. It became eventually the presidential palace of the future Napoleon III and is now the *Palais de l'Elysée*, residence of the President of the French Republic.

The Place Louis XV

The Louvre gardens were reshaped once again. On the great esplanade between the Tuileries swing bridge and the Cours-la-Reine, Gabriel created the Place Louis XV. It was octagonal in shape and bordered by a moat twenty metres wide, with a stone balustrade and spanned by bridges. At the eight corners of the octagon stood small pavilions housing steps leading to the flower-beds and lawns. At the centre of the square, a statue of the King by Bouchardon was erected in 1748. The *Pont de la Concorde* was completed in 1790 and the Marly Horses by Coustou were placed there in 1794.
At the north side of the square Gabriel built twin palaces, now the Crillon Hotel and the Automobile Club, leaving open the view towards the Seine. To the east of the Rue Royale was the Garde-Meuble de la Couronne where Marie Antoinette had a *pied-à-terre*; it became the Ministry of the Navy in 1792.
The Rue Royale, with its stone houses led to the *Eglise de la Madeleine*, completed under Louis-Philippe.

The Hôtel Royal and the Ecole Militaire

In 1750, west of the Hôtel des Invalides, beyond the village of Gros-Caillou, the banker Paris-Duverney, supported by that effective patron of the arts, Madame Pompadour, proposed to Louis XV the founding of a special school for the training of five hundred impoverished young gentlemen as army officers. The King was enthusiastic about the idea and the architect Jacques-Ange Gabriel drew up plans on a grand scale. The Ecole Militaire opened in 1760, and was reorganized and expanded in 1777 to include the *elite* of French provincial military schools as well. Napoleon Bonaparte was enrolled here at the age of 15;

when he left he was an artillery sub-lieutenant. The facade of the college overlooks the *Champ de Mars* which was used as a parade ground. Here the first experiments with balloons were made by the physicist Charles and the brothers Robert. During the Revolution, great crowds used its open space to assemble and demonstrate.

The Panthéon

During his serious illness in Metz in 1744, Louis XV vowed to rebuild the old Eglise Sainte-Geneviève, which had by then fallen into a bad state of repair. He appointed Soufflot as architect. Much criticized for his design, Soufflot died in 1780 just after building the street which bears his name. Various governments transformed the church, which is flanked by the Ecole de Droit and the adjoining Mairie of the 5th Arrondissement, into a necropolis for famous men; today called the *Panthéon*.

The Palais Bourbon

The Palais Bourbon was built during the reigns of Louis XV and Louis XVI and later enlarged to include the Hôtel de Lassay. Its entrance in the Rue de l'Université has remained unchanged and its gardens run down to the Seine where they meet the Pont Louis XVI built in 1787 by an engineer named Perronet. The Palace was confiscated during the Revolution to become the seat of the Council of Five Hundred; its facade was modified to match the Temple of Glory, which was later to become the Eglise de la Madeleine.

Gardens at the time of Louis XVI

Under Louis XVI, new buildings arose all over Paris, especially in the northern districts. The new mansions all had gardens: Landscape, English, Antique, even Chinese in style. Many of them were expropriated and opened to the public by the Revolution. The garden of the Palais-Royal was a great centre for amusements and was also a meeting place for those who conspired against the

The Palais du Luxembourg seen from the garden. It was built for Marie de Medici by Salomon de Brosse. Its gardens in the French style, embellished by stretches of water and fountains, open up the area as far as the Observatory. Today the Senate sits there.

Left Above: The Pantheon is the highest point on the Left Bank. It was built by Louis XV to replace the Eglise Saint-Geneviève, in gardens belong to the Abbey.

Left Below: The Rue Mouffetard cuts through the Latin Quarter. Originally a Roman road leading to Italy, it became the main street of the Bourg Saint-Médard. It is the continuation of the Rue Descartes and comes out in the Place de la Contrescarpe where the poets of the Pleiad used to meet.

The Rue de Rivoli, with its elegant arcades and houses, stretches from Saint-Germain-l'Auxerrois to the Place de la Concorde. Its buildings, with both front and back entrances, were often used for clandestine lovers' meetings.

Previous pages: The terraces of the Tuileries and the Museums of the Jeu de Paume and the Orangerie look down on the Place de la Concorde, designed by Gabriel for Louis XV. The Place de la Concorde is embellished by eight pavilions with statues representing the great cities of France, the Luxor Obelisk and monumental fountains.

Court. The Duc d'Antin replanted the Cours-la-Reine and the Champs-Elysées. At the top where the victims of the Saint Bartholomew massacre had been buried, he created avenues radiating outwards as from a star, to be known henceforth as the Etoile de Chaillot. The *Arc de Triomphe*, which was erected later, had already been planned under Louis XIV but it was Napoleon who, after his victory at Austerlitz, ordered it to be built to the west of the Etoile tollgate in the *Fermiers Généraux* wall. It was not actually inaugurated, however, until 1836, during the reign of Louis-Philippe. The names of the generals who fought for the Emperor, and their battles, were engraved on the inside walls.

The Revolution nationalizes the Church's properties and estates

To make up for the State's permanent deficit, the Revolution nationalized all the property of the Church, whose religious orders it had already abolished in November 1789. The Church had owned about an eighth of Paris and all of its land

was henceforth to belong to the State, together with property belonging to those who had fled to foreign countries, to those sentenced to death or imprisonment, to princes and to the royal family. The revolutionary committees and clubs gained power and mercilessly eliminated their enemies. Louis XVI was beheaded on 21 January 1793 and Marie-Antoinette followed him to the guillotine on 16 October of the same year. The *Commune* triumphed over the *Convention*. Then came the counter-revolution called *Thermidor* because it began on 9 Thermidor An II (27 July 1794).

From the Directoire to 18 Brumaire

After the revolutionary terror came the *Directoire*. The new rich jostled each other in the theatres, there was dancing and gambling everywhere and *restaurants* were the new fashion; there were two thousand in Paris, many of them opened by émigrés' former cooks, who were destined to be the founders of French gastronomy. The most luxurious restaurants were at the Palais

Royal, where dandies and fine ladies paraded in extravagant costumes.

The Revolution swept away the crafts and trade guilds. In their place, industry came to the capital: factories producing gunpowder, guns and fabrics, and a chemical and dye works set up at Javel by Comte d'Artois. In 1799 Philippe Lebon patented a process for making gas and Delessert set up a sugar beet refinery.

The Consulate and the Empire

The Empire was proclaimed on 18 May 1804. On 2 December, Napoleon crowned himself emperor at Notre-Dame in the presence of Pope Pius VII. Military etiquette and splendid uniforms were restored; field-marshals gave fashionable dinners; Talleyrand's receptions and supper parties were renowned. Many aristocrats returned to Paris and traditional festivities and military victories were celebrated once again. New streets such as the Rue de Rivoli and the Rue de Castiglione were laid out with arcades of white stone and with side streets leading up to the *Grands Boulevards*. The Rue de la Paix absorbed the medieval gardens of the Capucines.

The Restoration and the July Monarchy

The Restoration continued what the Empire had begun. Based on the London model, roofed in arcades of shops running between two streets

were built, the most famous example being the *Passage des Panoramas* near the Bourse. Theatres opened all around the Grands Boulevards. The *Canal Saint-Martin* was dug, the *Bourse* (the Stock Exchange) and the *Quartier de l'Europe* were completed.

The three-day revolution which put Louis-Philippe d'Orleans into power demonstrated the impossibility of preventing riots and barricades. But it was under Napoleon III that the building of the great avenues destined to completely alter the appearance of the capital were begun.

The Palais Bourbon, seat of the National Assembly, faces the Madeleine along the line of the Pont de la Concorde and echoes its classical columns. Their massiveness is possibly due to a changeover from the inch and toise to the metric system.

IMPERIAL PARIS

The Emperor's Plans

Europe was experiencing an unprecedented industrial and financial boom when Napoleon III was elected emperor on 2 December 1852. But Paris remained an inextricable tangle of buildings in a confusing labyrinth of streets. Even though public fountains were now quite numerous and water carriers delivered to upper floors, the streets of Old Paris had scarcely changed since the Middle Ages, and their stinking open gutters still emptied into the Seine; there were no drains.

And yet in a few years, through the determination of the Emperor, ably seconded by Baron Haussmann, the capital became the City of Light, "Paris, Queen of the World", a legend that has conquered the world through the paintings of the Impressionists, the poems of Baudelaire and the photographs of Nadar.

The Empire was a period of splendour. The Court was rejuvenated. The Imperial family settled at the Tuileries, but in summer preferred the quiet and intimate atmosphere of the Château de Saint-Cloud, near to the capital. Fontainebleau and Compiègne were much favoured by the society of the time as country retreats. In Paris, the reign of Louis-Philippe had seen the laying out of the Grands Boulevards. Napoleon III saw himself as an imperial builder and the great avenues of the capital which he helped create clearly met a strategic concern.

The Emperor, author of *The Abolition of Poverty*, concerned himself with improving the condition

Above: The Arc de Triomphe lit up on 14 July, Bastille Day, the folds of the French flag shimmering in the flood-lights.

Left; From the Carrousel the extraordinary fore-shortened view through the Tuileries Gardens. Right in the middle, the Obelisk at the Place de la Concorde and the Arc de Triomphe at the Etoile.

of the working classes. Some 1500 architects and a veritable army of 60,000 workmen helped to modernize Paris, giving it more or less its present dimensions and the framework for its future development.

In memory of London Parks

The Emperor dreamt of creating parks in Paris similar to those with lakes, cascades and buildings, that he had admired during his exile in London. Haussmann, with the assistance of Charles Alphand, designed the *Bois de Boulogne*, the *Bois de Vincennes* and the parks of *Buttes-Chaumont, Montsouris* and *Monceau*. At the same time the Baron also extended the Rue de Rivoli in the direction of the Hôtel de Ville so that it met the Boulevard de Sebastapol at Châtelet. While Alphand designed the felicitous landscapes of the capital, the engineer Eugene Belgrand was made responsible for making the city a healthier place. In fact, cholera was still a threat and underground tunnels or sewers were badly needed for drainage.

The Baltard umbrellas

In the centre of Paris stood Les Halles, the belly of Paris as Emile Zola called it, a colourful market which nevertheless posed tremendous problems of supply and circulation in this working class district. Belgrand had them demolished and replaced by Baltard's Parapluies (umbrellas), pavilions of open frame construction in iron and cast

61

iron. When they were finally demolished in 1969, American museums turned out to be more interested in them than the Parisians themselves. Of the twelve original parapluies only one remains, at Nogent-sur-Marne a few miles from the capital.

A network of new projects spread from the Place de l'Etoile as far as the Trocadéro. The Chaillot area took its present form in 1866, extending to the Pont de l'Alma, famous for the statute of a Zouave (soldier) at the base of one of its piers. Whenever the Seine is in flood, Parisians can measures its rise by the depth to which this gallant soldier is submerged. When the bridge was recently rebuilt, the Zouave was kept in response to public pressure.

One of the most splendid achievements of Baron Haussmann was the thoroughfare now called *Avenue Foch*. After ascending the Champs-Elysées with its magnificent mansions to the Arc de Triomphe at the Etoile, an equally fine road was needed to reach the restored Bois de Boulogne. Originally called the Avenue de l'Imperatrice, it very soon became the most elegant drive in the capital.

The Emperor's favourite, Haussmann, also played a glittering role in the fashionable life of the capital in which a succession of foreign kings, princes and heads of state participated, ensuring a livelihood for all manner of craftsmen.

Haute couture, as we know it, was just beginning. The English *couturier* Worth dressed the Empress and ladies of the Court in the low-cut graceful dresses depicted in Winterhalter's paintings. In interior decoration, the Empress Eugenie brought the Louis XVI style back into fashion although gradually it was made cumbersome by padded velvet armchairs and sofas, matched with heavy curtains protecting opulent new houses

Above: The Parc Monceau, its ruins recalling romantic landscapes by Hubert Robert. It was one of the great parks which Napoleon III had refashioned in the style of those he had known in London.

Left: The Place Vendôme matches its classic octagonal form to the column overlooking it, cast in bronze from guns captured by Napoleon at Austerlitz. Here and in the Rue de la Paix the grand Paris jewellers are to be found.

The Opéra at the top of the avenue that bears its name, glittering with gilt, marble and porphyry, is the work of the architect Charles Garnier and was built in the Napoleon III style. It has an enormous stage which will take 450 performers.

against draughts. These trends are also to be found in Garnier's opera house.

The 1855 World Fair

Five million visitors attended the World Fair which opened in 1855; twenty thousand exhibitors showed their latest products in the Palace of Industry on the Champs-Elysees.. The visitors came from all parts of the world, and included Queen Victoria who arrived at the Strasburg Station (now the Gare de l'Est), recently rebuilt to match the scale of the boulevard which was cut through the Left Bank as far as the Avenue de l'Observatoire. It took its name from the *Fontaine*

de Davioud in the Place Saint-Michel, and is now known as the "Boul'Mich".

Everybody wanted to visit the sites of Imperial Paris. So Baron Haussmann started a cheap public transport system covering the city which allowed people to leave their own districts for work or entertainment – a real revolution. Some had a top deck reserved for men; their introduction into the life of the capital inspired savage cartoons.

Eighteen fifty-six was a particularly happy year; the *Prince Imperial* was born and the Crimean War was won. *Longchamp* race course and the nearby *Grand Cascade* in the *Bois de Boulogne* attracted elegant crowds; the additions to the Louvre were completed by 3000 workmen.

The Pont Alexandre III was dedicated to the Czar during the visit of his son Nicolas II. It is a typical 1900-style monument, lavish and over-decorated. It has a single metal span and its decorated pillars are crowned by allegorical figures and gilded statues of Pegasus.

Below The Orsay Museum, on the site of the former hotel of the Orsay Palace and the Paris-Orléans-Riviera station, houses XIXth century collections, from the "pompous" ("pompiers") to the post-impressionists. The glass wall decorations have been inspired by those created by Hector Guimard for the Paris metro; its animals and allegoric figures of bronze decorated the Trocadéro Palace.

On an economic level the cost of all the demolitions began to be felt: rents rose as new buildings replaced old ones, forcing craftsmen and workmen to move to the suburbs.

Paris doubles in size

The huge building works undertaken all over the city led to the absorption of rural districts on the city's boundaries into Paris, which doubled in size, reaching 7802 hectares. Its population, spread over twenty arrondissements, similarly expanded to about 1,700,000.

Napoleon III began the *Boulevard Malesherbes* where the *Eglise Saint-Augustin* was built by Baltard, in iron and cast-iron. The vista took in the Monceau plain and park. The gilded gates, which restrict access to the riverside mansions, are beautiful examples of the wrought ironwork of the period.

Eighteen sixty-two was a great year for theatres. The foundation stone of the Opéra was laid, the Châtelet (the present Théâtre Musical de Paris) was completed, and the facade of the Comédie-Française was renewed. In fact the stage played a very important role in the life of the city at this time – as the saucy refrains of Offenbach's operettas underlined.

But far and away the largest building site was the Cite, a working class area teeming with life. From Notre-Dame to the Place Dauphine everything was torn down, making a desert around the cathedral square. Notre-Dame was restored by Viollet-le-Duc in the Gothic style, made popular by Victor Hugo.

On the Left Bank the *Boulevard Saint-Germain* stretched from the Chambre des Deputés to the Halle-aux-Vins. The digging up of *Rue Monge* uncovered the *Arenes de Lutèce* and other Gallo-Roman remains. Boulevard Raspail was laid out in the direction of the Barrière d'Enfer where, at the Place Denfert-Rochereau, Ledoux's city toll houses and the entrance to the catacombs can still be seen. The *Rue de Rennes* linked the Montparnasse railway station to Saint-Germain-des-Prés.

Department stores multiplied. The Trois Quartiers, specializing in new lines, had already been built during the Restoration, while the first of the new stores was Bon Marché built by Aristide

The Eiffel Tower: One of the three most visited monuments in Paris. When the weather is fine you can see a distance of 90 kilometres. It was erected in two years by the engineer Gustave Eiffel, and was the main attraction of the 1889 World Fair. During recent restoration, its garlands of decorative iron work were removed and sold to collectors.

Entrance to the Porte Dauphine Metro station, with its glass canopy, in typical 1900 Art Nouveau style. The decorative green cast ironwork above ground gives way to ceramic tiling embellished with irises along the passages and platforms.

Boucicaut between the present Rue de Sèvres and the Rue de Babylon; it pioneered a whole new system of retailing.

Photography: a new eye

Photography, invented by Niepce and Daguerre, became madly popular overnight. Nadar, the most famous photographer of the mid-19th century (he was also an aeronaut, a journalist and a cartoonist), was a bold pioneer of this new art. During a trip in a balloon, he took the first aerial photograph of Paris. He also took photographs in the catacombs and the sewers by artificial light. His postcard views of the city are now collectors' items.

The Commune de Paris and the Third Republic

The apparent success of the World Fair hid troubles to come: the war with Prussia, the fall of the Empire and the continuation of hostilities by the Government of National Defence, subjecting hunger-stricken Paris to the rigours of a siege during the terrible winter of 1870-71. Surrender was followed by the Commune, which unleashed destruction upon the capital. Before it was cruelly suppressed by the "Versaillais" government, the Hôtel de Ville, the Tuileries and whole streets were set on fire and the column in Place Vendôme pulled down.

Reviving a pre-war project, the National Assembly voted to build a church on the hill of Montmartre by public subscription. Gothic ideas gave way to a basilica in the Romano-Byzantine style with white cupolas of local stone rising in the Paris sky. The Butte Montmartre being crumbly and full of hollows, foundations thirty-eight metres in depth were necessary, sunk in eighty-three shafts lined with masonry and linked by supporting arches.

The Hôtel de Ville was rebuilt in the Renaissance style to four times its previous size.

Under the Third Republic, new World Fairs left their mark on the capital. In 1878 Davioud's Trocadéro was built on the top of the Chaillot hill. The

67

Right: The Sacré-Coeur, a Romano-Byzantine basilica dominating Paris, the roofs of the houses on the Butte Montmartre clinging to its sides. Its history merges with that of Paris: Saint Denis and his companions were beheaded on its site; and Henry IV occupied it.

Below: The steps of the Rue Foyatier alongside the Montmartre Funicular. The highest point in Paris (129 metres), Montmartre is known for its windmills, its rustic cafés, and its Bohemianism. Berlioz, Renoir, Utrillo and Raoul Dufy lived there.

Parc de Montsouris was opened in the new Rue de Tolbiac district near the Porte d'Italie and the Opéra, a typical Napoleon III monument, was covered with gilt, coloured marble and porphyry. The new Ministry of Foreign Affairs was built on the Quai d'Orsay.

The Eiffel Tower

The Eiffel Tower remains today one of the three main attractions in Paris, the other two being Notre-Dame and the Beaubourg Centre. On a clear day visibility is 90 kilometres. Built by the engineer Gustave Eiffel in two years, the tower comprises 12,000 pieces of metal and 2,500,000 rivets. Its weight is 7000 tons, supported by masonry at the four corners and it has three platforms, the highest being topped by a pavilion with bell tower. It can be ascended by stairs or lift. Today only the Montparnasse Tower is taller.

1900: Art Nouveau and the Metro

The 1900 World Fair attracted 5,859,955 visitors, an all-time record. A contest was held six years earlier to select the architects for the two exhibition halls to be built at right angles to the Seine – the *Grand Palais* and the *Petit Palais*.
During the visit of Czar Nicolas II of Russia, a cast-iron bridge opposite the Invalides was dedicated to his father, the Czar Alexander III.

running during the exhibition from Porte Maillot to the Porte de Vincennes. The station steps had cast-iron stair rails and lamp standards decorated in an exuberant floral manner which the disrespectful were quick to christen "spaghetti style". But the Art Nouveau style remains vigorous; for example, when Pierre Cardin bought *Maxim's* restaurant he opened branches all over the world, furnished and equipped exactly like the original one in the Rue Royale.

Manet and Degas depicted in their paintings and drawings aspects of the *vie parisienne*, from the Opéra to the Folies-Bergères, while Toulouse-Lautrec painted life in the brothels in down-to-earth style. Many of their works can be seen at the *Musée du Jeu de Paume* and the *Orangerie*.

The Third Republic continued the work of Haussmann on a more modest scale.

The First World War

Paris was saved in 1914 by General Gallieni who requisitioned all the capital's taxis to take reinforcements to the battle of the Marne at Nanteuille-Haudouin. In 1917 the Russian Revolution changed the fate of the world, and was followed by revolutions in Germany and Austria. On 11 November 1918 the Armistice was signed.

Below: Footbridge over the Saint Martin canal, one of three in the northern and eastern parts of the capital, the others being Saint Denis and Ourcq. Their sandy and shady banks, formerly towpaths, are safe and pleasant cycle tracks.

PARIS TODAY

A New World

At the end of the war in 1918, the world had radically changed. In effect, the Second Empire had ended with the *Belle Epoque* and the 19th century with the outbreak of the First World War. Living conditions had now changed irreversibly. During the hostilities, women had replaced men in their usual occupations and had become more self-assured and independent. They were no longer passive and their model became the "businesswoman". In Paris, Chanel took over from Poiret.

Post-war France dressed its wounds and Paris began to live again. At the Theatre des Champs-Elysées in the Avenue Montaigne, built between 1911 and 1913 by Perret in a very sober style, the Ballets Russes electrified the town, their seductive Slav charm affecting all around them. Montparnasse displaced Montmartre as the intellectual centre of the capital, with La Coupole as its most famous meeting place.

In strong reaction against the "spaghetti style", Mallet-Stevens created functional architecture, and his metal-framed buildings with large bay windows can still be seen in the street that bears his name. Le Courbusier built his first terrace-roofed houses on stilts, and also designed the Swiss pavilion of the Cité Universitaire, behind the Parc Montsouris, which was to receive students from all over the world.

As a result of new media such as radio and cinema, new ideas in cultural and artistic fields spread very rapidly. At the same time the motorcar began

The Great Arch, designed by the architect Paul Andreu and inaugurated by President Mitterrand in July 1990, forms the culminating point of the Defence perspective, one of the first sites built in glass and steel. This office complex is composed of multiple skyscrapers.

Left: The Forum des Halles has three underground levels. Under its glass-roofs and around its terraces, are a multitude of shops, restaurants and croissant bars.

the progress which would lead to its displacing the train after the Second World War. An increase in the number of women's magazines fostered a growth and popularization of ideas in fashion and interior decoration.

The Decorative Arts

The cinema was the invention of the Lumière brothers and the first films were shown in the Indian Room at the Grand Café, as a memorial plaque at 14 Boulevard des Capucines records. The first talkie, *The Jazz Singer*, conquered the capital in 1927.

In the fields of art and literature the twenties were a very rich period indeed. The theatre was a potent attraction in the life of Paris with famous actors such as Sacha Guitry, Gaston Baty, Jacques Copeau, Louis Jouvet, Charles Dullin, Georges and Ludmilla Pitoeff. The novels of Charles Maurras, Francois Mauriac, Paul Morand, André Maurois, Jean Giraudoux and Jules Romains were avidly bought. Saxophones and clarinets gave out the furious shock waves of New Orleans jazz.

All these trends came to a climax in the Exhibition of Decorative Arts which Le Corbusier called "the international marathon of the domestic arts"; it brought together artists, manufacturers, architects and craftsmen skilled in building, paper making, textiles and ceramics. Black and burnt orange were fashionable colours for interior decoration and for furniture, the latter in geometric shapes and lacquered to reflect the light.

The refined simplicity of this environment called

for feminine fashions to match. Vigorous dances, such as the Charleston and Black Bottom, led to a fashion for short waistless dresses, short hair and cloche hats worn low on the forehead. Chanel was the leader of fashion and remained so for nearly half a century.

The splendid buildings of the Avenues Matignon and Montaigne and the residential quarter to the west bear witness to the geometric style in their balconies, facades and monumental entrance halls. Women participated in the *concours d'élégance* for cars and soon took to the driver's seat.

Between the wars there were some forty rival makes without counting the coach builders. Citroen put an illuminated sign on the Eiffel Tower and Renault followed it into the small car market while continuing to specialize in its famous red and black Model G7 taxis.

In 1931 the Colonial Exhibition was held at the Porte de Vincennes, introducing the arts and crafts of five continents to the capital. It later became the Museum of African and Pacific Arts.

The International Exhibition of 1937

The 1937 International Exhibition of Arts and Techniques was held at the Palais de Chaillot on a site sloping down from the Trocadéro to the Seine, opposite the Ecole Militaire. On the top of the hill an esplanade, site of firework displays, was laid out, flanked by two exhibition halls in a crescent shape, with steps descending to the river and enclosing splendid fountains and neat gardens. At the exhibition Parisians saw their first television sets. The building on the Passy side houses the Musée de la Marine and the Musée de l'Homme, the other wing the Musée des Monuments Français and the Cinematheque film library. The Musée d'Art Moderne de la Ville de Paris occupies the Palais de Tokyo near the Place de l'Alma.

The Palais de Chaillot built on the levelled hillside by the Place de Trocadéro for the 1937 Exhibition of Arts and Techniques. Its giant esplanade opposite the Eiffel Tower is an ideal spot for firework displays.

The Second World War

Paris was declared an open city and occupied by the German Army in June 1940. Vichy became the capital of the country. Parisians suffered difficult times with round-ups and arrests. Bicycles became the common means of transport and delivery tricycles replaced taxis. The town was liberated in August 1944: the Leclerc division, the US Army and General de Gaulle entered Paris to general rejoicing. The German surrender was signed on 8 May, 1945.

The Motorcar devours Paris

During the war most of the road and rail bridges around the capital had been destroyed. After 1945, they were quickly rebuilt thanks partly to Marshall Aid. The population of the city increased, new building resumed followed by the development of residential suburbs, and new towns on geometric lines were built over wheatfields to the north and west of the capital.

Haute couture revived as soon as wartime restrictions disappeared. Christian Dior's "New Look" was exported all over the world in 1947 and he was followed by young new designers such as Pierre Balmain, Jacques Fath, Balenciaga and Givenchy. In the sixties Yves Saint-Laurent, André Courrèges and Philippe Venet began the new trend to ready-to-wear clothes and men's fashions and accelerated the move into the perfume business.

The Boulevard Périphérique

Renault brought out its 4CV (4 horse-power) car in 1947, followed by Citroen with its 2CV, a utility version of the convertible. Easy credit and a general improvement in living standards brought the car within reach of everyone. The result was enormous traffic jams when offices closed. The city pavements lost their trees, their "green lungs", and were invaded by the motorcar. To relieve the congestion, the Boulevard Périphérique was begun in 1957, a thirty-five-kilometre ring road without a single traffic light which enabled cars to avoid seventy crossroads on the boulevards. The most spectacular interchanges are at the Porte de la Chapelle in the direction of Le Bourget, the Porte de Bagnolet linking Charles-de-Gaulle Airport and the capital, and the Porte de

The Maine-Montparnasse Tower on the Left Bank. It includes an important commercial centre, a sports complex, a pavement which serves unofficially as a rink for roller skaters, and is linked with the Montparnasse station by gardens.

The Parc des Buttes-Chaumont was part of the village of la Villette, which was absorbed by the city in 1860. This village of wheatfields and vineyards saw the carriages of Louis XVI and his family go by in their flight to Varennes and on their return to Paris.

The Maison de la Radio, on the Right Bank, Avenue du Président Kennedy. It is a white circular building with a white tower. In the background, the village of Auteuil, which existed before the Roman Conquest. Boileau lived in Auteuil, and Molière may have been buried there.

Bercy which connects with the A4 motorway. A whole network of crossovers has also been built to lessen bottlenecks in the south and west. A suspension bridge, the only one of its type in Paris, spans the lines at Austerlitz station.

La Défense

Postwar construction took many forms but was on a cautious scale at first to protect Old Paris. For example, the fine group of UNESCO buildings were not allowed to mar the proportions of the Ecole Militaire. To the west, on a large tract of undeveloped land on the Champs-Elysées/Porte Maillot axis, the new Quartier de la Défense, was started in 1970 and linked with Saint-Germain-en-Laye by a line of the RER (réseau express regional).

The CNIT exhibition hall in concrete, steel and glass covers a triangular site of 90,000 square metres, its arched roof supported at only three points. A veritable Manhattan of office blocks has been built around a huge paved area adorned with fountains, with an underground shopping centre to match.

The Maison de la Radio

The Maison de la Radio, soon nicknamed the "Gruyere Palace", stands on the Quai Kennedy near the Pont Mirabeau (16e). It is indeed shaped like a piece of cheese, with a white tower in the centre. Across the Seine, sixteen tower blocks on stilts, with three levels for vehicle and pedestrian traffic, have been built on a former industrial area fronting the river.

The Maine-Montparnasse Tower

The Maine-Montparnasse project is part of a great plan for urban renewal around Montparnasse station, designed to make a focus of attention on the Left Bank to balance the Quartier de la Défense across the river. The Tower, which has fifty-six floors of offices with restaurants offering panoramic views at the top, is surrounded by other tall buildings, a paved area, small gardens and shopping centres. The departure hall of the rebuilt station is decorated with large wall paintings by Vasarely.

The Beaubourg Centre

In the Beaubourg quarter the Centre National d'Art et de Culture Georges Pompidou with its glass walls and giant pipes painted in primary colours, has given a new youthful appearance to an old medieval site. The area has been rebuilt and fashion boutiques and art galleries have opened around the Centre, which represents a new museum concept. The aim is not to preserve

works of art but to bring them to life, and to interest a wide public of young people in the artistic creations of our time.

This has met with considerable success; since its opening in 1977 the Centre has had over six million visitors, becoming, with the Eiffel Tower and Notre-Dame, one of the three most popular attractions of the capital. The brainchild of the late President Pompidou, its construction began in 1972 on a site between the Rue de Renard and the Rue Rambuteau. It covers 103,000 square metres and is 166 metres long, 60 metres wide and 42 metres high. From its escalators visitors get a remarkable view over Paris.

Grouping together the various strands of modern culture in a single building, the Centre seeks to break out of the sense of isolation which often prevails in traditional museums. Admission to some parts, such as the library, is free. The escalators offer a kind of architectural tour; the service ducts appear as decorations hung on the framework of the building. Spread over five stories, the Centre comprises the National Museum of Modern Art, the Industrial Design Centre (whose exhibitions are very popular), a Public Reference Library, the Institute for Contemporary Acoustic and Musical Research, together with a collection of drawings and a branch of the National Film Library.

In front of the building there is a large bowl-shaped open space and there are streets restricted to pedestrians, giving easy access to the complex.

The "Trou" des Halles

In 1969 Les Halles, the central markets which had for so long occupied the same site close by the church of Saint-Eustache, were transferred to the suburbs, to Rungis near Orly. Baltard's pavilions were demolished and an enormous hole was excavated which various projects will eventually fill. Along the line of the Rue Pierre Lescot the RER joins up with the Metro network above which the Forum des Halles has been built on three levels around a small terrace, with shops, cinemas and car parks.

The Lake in the Bois de Boulogne, crowded with rowing boats in the summer. The Bagatelle gardens are famous for their rose gardens in June.

The Bastille Opera House, inaugurated in 1990, designed by the architect Carlos Ott, was to make available the latest in acoustics to as wide a public as possible. Its pure, rounded lines are in the same shades of grey and white as those used for the inside architecture. The monumental staircase is in hommage to Charles Garnier's Paris Opera House.

Right: One of the great Paris attractions: the escalators and exterior walkways at the Beaubourg Centre. Free admission to many of its events has encouraged attendances.

Sport in Paris

The main sports ground are to be found on the outskirts of Paris. The great crowds of football and rugby fans congregate at the Parc des Princes near the Porte de Saint-Cloud. Pope John Paul II celebrated mass there for 60,000 youngsters. The recently opened multi-purpose stadium at Bercy in the east of the city only seats 17,000.

The venue for tennis is the Roland Garros stadium near the Porte d'Auteuil which has new courts and attracts crowds in proportion to the two million people who play tennis in France. The race-courses are wonderfully situated: flat racing at Longchamp, steeplechasing at Auteuil, and trotting races at Vincennes. Each October the Prix de l'Arc-de-Triomphe at Longchamp attracts large numbers of British visitors.

Recent Changes

The Musée du XIXᵉ Siecle is being laid out in the buildings of the Orsay hotel and station by the Seine, and the former abattoirs at La Villette are being converted to house the Musée des Sciences et Techniques. The Pavillon de Marsan of the Musée des Arts Decoratifs is becoming a museum of costume.

INDEX

ACKNOWLEDGEMENTS

The publishers would like to thank the following for their invaluable help and co-operation : Mlle Anne Dorffer, from the Direction Générale de la Communication de la Mairie de Paris ; Mlle Anne Voisin and M. Grenier, of the Conseil Régional d'Ile-de-France. The author would also like to thank Mme Renée Plouin and MM. André Chastel, René Héron de Villefosse, Jacques Hillairet, Pierre Ordioni, Marc Ambroise-Rendu, Emmanuel de Roux and Pierre-André Touttain whose work on Paris and whose advice were of enormous help.